KEYS TO
GOD'S GRACE
The Hidden Joy of Prayer,
Fasting and Almsgiving

Jeff Smith

the WORD
among us

The Word Among Us Press

9639 Doctor Perry Road

Ijamsville, Maryland 21754

ISBN: 0-932085-33-4

Cover design by Christopher Ranck

Contents

Introduction

Every day, God invites us to experience him more deeply through prayer and repentance. The words he spoke to King Solomon centuries ago resound just as powerfully to us today: "If my people who are called by my name humble themselves, pray and seek my face, and turn from their wicked ways, then I will hear from heaven, and forgive their sin and heal their land" (2 Chronicles 7:14).

When we hear a message like this, we can react in one of two ways. We can feel that it's too harsh and demanding, or we can recognize in it the heart of a loving Father. God wants us to know how much he wants to fill us with his grace and favor. Every day, he cries out to each of us, "Come to me because I love you. I want to heal you. Let my light cast out the darkness in your heart."

In this book we have focused on the traditional practices of prayer, almsgiving, and fasting. In every age, countless Christians have been drawn to these practices because they found that through these "doors," they entered a place in their relationship with God where mercy and grace abound. It is our prayer that as you respond to God's call to prayer, repentance, and generosity, you too will enter a place of deep blessing from the Lord.

Jesus is waiting each day, longing to hear from you and—even more important—eager to speak to you. And, when you hear the voice of the Lord in your heart, your entire life can be changed.

Jeff Smith
The Word Among Us

"I Miss You"

When Fr. Mark first became a priest, he was so in love with Jesus that he would often spend hours before the Lord in prayer every day. But once he became pastor of a large suburban parish, he began to feel crushed by the responsibility. On his best days, he would spare only a little time to be with the Lord—and even those times were dominated by pleas for financial help for the parish and anxious fretting over the latest personality clashes among his parishioners.

Gradually, an elderly woman who was a long-time member of the parish began to notice how tired Fr. Mark was looking and how labored his homilies had become. She began praying for him, and after a week or so, she approached him. "Fr. Mark," she said, "God told me to tell you something." Knowing that she was a prayerful woman, he invited her into his office, sat down, and listened intently. "Maybe God has finally answered my prayer for money," he thought. But, rather than reveal a new source of financing, she said, "Jesus wants you to know that he misses spending time with you."

Fr. Mark was stunned. With those few, simple words, he saw how distant he had grown from the Lord. He began again to set aside a few hours every morning for prayer and Mass. He arranged to tend to his duties in the afternoons and evenings and delegated some of the tasks he

had recently accepted. Sure enough, the love that Fr. Mark had felt for Jesus in the early years of his priesthood began to revive. What's more, some of the financial and relationship problems his parish was experiencing began to diminish.

"I miss you." How heart-breaking these words sound when spoken by God! For centuries, he has been imploring his children to spend time with him in prayer, and people as diverse as powerful bishops and lowly peasants have responded to his call. Augustine the orator; Bernard of Clairvaux the statesman; Catherine of Siena the dreamer; Elizabeth Ann Seton the housewife; Ignatius Loyola the soldier—all these and countless others spent hours a day in God's presence, and they grew soft and pliable as they let the Lord teach them.

At the Home of Martha and Mary

One of the most moving gospel stories about the need for prayer is Luke's story of Martha and Mary (Luke 10:38-42). These two sisters lived with their brother Lazarus in the town of Bethany, and Jesus had come to love them as his own family (John 11:1-3,35-36).

On one occasion, Jesus visited their home, and Martha invited him to stay for dinner. As she busied herself preparing the meal, Mary sat at Jesus' feet soaking in his teaching. Martha noticed this and grew agitated at Mary's apparent laziness. Finally, she blurted out, "Lord, do you not care that my sister has left me to serve alone? Tell her to help me" (Luke 10:40). Jesus' response was far different from what Martha expected. "Martha, Martha," he said, "you are anxious and troubled about many things; one thing is needful.

Mary has chosen the good portion, which shall not be taken away from her" (10:41-42).

The Church—Sitting at Jesus' Feet

Why did Jesus take such delight in Mary? Because, in her humility, she had made herself available to him. In Mary, Jesus found an open heart to whom he could bare his soul. Free of the burdens and debates that he often faced with Pharisees and scribes, he could speak as honestly with Mary as he did with the Twelve. He could tell her about his love for Israel and his Father's desire to save his people. Since the cross was already on his mind (Luke 9:22), he could tell her about his death and resurrection. Such an open exchange must have been a source of great joy for Jesus.

In her humble disposition and her willingness

to be taught by Jesus, Mary is a symbol of the church, the bride of Christ. How Jesus longs to see his church take Mary's place at his feet! He knows that it's when we fix our attention on him that we are transformed. The same intimacy with Jesus that Mary knew is available to all of us, but it only comes as we seek him in quiet, personal prayer and in the corporate prayer of the liturgy. Like Mary, we can bring great joy to Jesus' heart. He delights in pouring out grace upon a church that has adopted a humble, teachable attitude.

Martha: Anxious and Concerned

Martha loved Jesus, too. Like her sister, she had come to believe in him and looked forward to whatever time he could spend with them. How was it possible, then, for Martha to have

become so upset with Mary and to have missed out on the blessings of being at Jesus' feet?

Jesus could tell that Martha wasn't concerned only about the dinner. "Many things" were on her mind—so many anxieties and frustrations, in fact, that she failed to respond to the heavenly reality in her midst. Just as Mary gives us one image of the church, so Martha provides another. Like Martha, we may be tempted to become preoccupied with all the pressing needs that the church faces. The poor and homeless cry out for help; many people have yet to hear the gospel; the sanctity of human life must be defended. We can become so busy trying to answer all these needs that we lose sight of the Master who longs to visit our home and give us a share in his heart.

To each of us, Jesus poses the same question that he asked Martha: "Are you so concerned

with what must be done that you cannot sit with me and receive my love? This is the 'one thing' that is 'needful.' This is the 'good portion' that will fill your heart with love for others. Without it, your service to me will end in frustration, bitterness, and emptiness." Jesus' words to us are an invitation to a deeper relationship with him. Though so many racing thoughts clouded her mind, Martha eventually became a disciple ruled by the Spirit. The same can happen to us; Jesus never stops inviting people to sit with him.

The Renewal of the Mind

At one time or another, many of us have experienced some sense of God's presence and love for us. It may have been at Mass, or it may have been in the quiet of our rooms. God became very real to us, and our hearts

were warmed by his love. However, after such a moving experience, the anxieties of life can very easily cloud our memories and rob our peace.

Why is this? Very often, the problem is that our hearts may have been touched by God's love, but our minds remain in need of renewal—something that can only happen by the power of the cross. As we sit at the feet of Jesus and gaze upon his cross, God will shine his light on the thoughts, desires, and assumptions within us that displease him. In the light of the love that Jesus poured out at Calvary, we will see our sin in a clearer way, and we will begin to take on a new way of thinking and acting.

God wants to change our minds as we "fight the good fight of the faith" (1 Timothy 6:12) and gaze prayerfully upon the cross. Make no mistake: Such prayer is very difficult at times, and

it will require some sacrifice on our part. But it is worth it as the Lord exposes our old ways of thinking and replaces them with his way of mercy, compassion, and obedience.

Imagine a young boy with his parents. At three years old, he begins to choose for himself. Sometimes, he is on the right path. At other times, he deviates from the path, and his parents must correct him lovingly but firmly. So too, as we sit at the foot of the cross, God will reveal those thoughts that must go. He will begin to tear down anger, fear, impurity, and self-righteousness and replace them with his peace, love, and self-control.

What About You?

As she took Jesus' rebuke to heart, Martha's life was gradually changed. She came to acknowledge

Jesus as "the Christ, the Son of God" and held firm trust in him even in the face of loss and sorrow (John 11:22,27). She continued to serve at her home (12:2), but freed from the anxiety and racing concerns that had dominated her previously. Over time, Martha learned to sit at Jesus' feet and hear from him.

Jesus is inviting all of us to sit before him. When we can't find the time to make it to Mass or to spend time alone with him, the Lord wants to say to us, "I really miss you. I want to reveal my heart to you." Jesus can be as present in our homes as he was in Martha's home. Let's take the time to be with him and listen.

Giving Our Whole Heart
to Jesus

We might think that, during Jesus' time, the atmosphere in the temple was always somber and quiet, but in fact, it was quite the opposite. On ordinary days, hundreds of worshippers made their way to the house of the Lord, and on special feasts like Passover, the numbers could swell into the thousands. Entire families came together to make their offerings of grain, fruit, and flocks. At unpredictable intervals, the air would be filled with the cries of a baby boy being circumcised.

The hymns and prayers of the faithful mingled with the bleating of sheep and the lowing of cattle to be offered as sacrifices. And, above all the din hovered the haze of incense.

It was in this atmosphere that Jesus spent the days before his death teaching anyone who would listen. Recounting one such day, St. Mark describes both the controversy and the admiration that Jesus evoked from his listeners. Chief priests and elders tried to intimidate him (Mark 11:28), and Pharisees sought to trap him in his words (12:13). These confrontations must have wearied the Lord. He wanted to spend his remaining time telling the crowd about his coming death, and yet he was constantly having to ward off the objections of his opponents.

Near the end of this day, Jesus—probably tired from the debates—sat down with his disciples to rest. As he surveyed the crowd, he

saw a host of people lined up to offer their temple tithe. There, amidst all the wealthy people offering large sums of money, Jesus noticed an elderly woman dressed in widow's clothing offering her own gift: "two copper coins, which are worth a penny" (Mark 12:42). Struck by this woman's poverty yet love for the Lord, Jesus told his disciples that she had given more than anyone else. "For all of them have contributed out of their abundance; but she out of her poverty has put in everything she had, all she had to live on" (12:44).

Why This Widow?

It is difficult for us to understand the plight of many widows in ancient Israel. Inheritances were not structured like they are today. When a Jewish man died, his entire inheritance passed

to his oldest son, leaving his widow dependent upon her child's generosity. While the son might be expected to give his mother a small portion, it didn't always happen. Consequently, widows could be left destitute—impoverished and defenseless.

In Jesus' day, many poor, devout widows must have frequented the temple. Why did this woman impress Jesus so much? Her clothes probably revealed how poor she was, but it wasn't just her poverty that moved Jesus. He could see into a person's heart, and he saw something that set her apart—an extravagant love for God that demonstrated itself in generosity. This widow lived in oppressive poverty, and yet she didn't blame God for her situation. She did not lose herself in bitterness or despair. Instead, she trusted enough in God's loving care to give him her last penny.

What's more, she wasn't embarrassed by her state. Her faith in God and her desire to give him everything was stronger than any sense of inferiority she may have felt as she stood next to the wealthy. Even though she probably had to beg for her next meal, her one goal at that moment was to give her all to God. When she presented those two precious coins, Jesus saw humility and trust in God for everything, even her survival.

The Church—Dependent on the Lord

In some ways, this widow represents the church. She had no one but God to love and care for her. She knew that without him, her life was hopeless. Her humble heart and her trust in God compelled her to give everything to the One she loved. As she made her offering, we

can just imagine the Spirit of God filling her with a heart of humility and generosity.

As the church, we too can know the touch of a God who is never stingy. All he asks is that we acknowledge that we are empty and destitute without him, and that we place no other loves before him. Day after day, Jesus looks to his bride to see if she has a humble and generous heart. Does she acknowledge that she cannot survive one day apart from her husband? As a member of the church—as part of the bride of Christ—do you have this kind of love for Jesus? Are your love for him and your surrender to him growing and deepening?

When God looks at us, he peers into every thought, every desire, and every priority that we hold dear. He sees and is pleased with the love we have for our spouse, our families, and our friends. He knows how dutifully we try

to fulfill the responsibilities of our lives. But most importantly, he wants to see how deeply we are in love with Jesus. This is the call of the gospel—to love God with all of our strength, all of our hearts, all of our minds, and all of our souls (Mark 12:30). Jesus invites us into a love relationship with him that is so passionate that even the great love we have for our family pales in comparison.

Sacrificial Giving

As our love for God grows, it should be reflected in our generosity toward him and his people—just as the widow demonstrated her love by her offering. The gift of two copper coins revealed the priorities of her heart: She loved God and she loved the temple in which he dwelt. Similarly, the way we spend our money reveals our priorities and love.

Over the past decade, scandals in different churches and charitable organizations have caused many Christians to shy away from the call to give generously. But scripture teaches that it is an honor and a privilege to participate in the building-up of the kingdom of God. In the Old Testament, God's people were commanded to offer ten percent of all their goods and income. Some New Testament communities went even further. In Jerusalem, for example, the first Christians pooled all of their goods together so that everyone was cared for.

How can we expect the gospel to be proclaimed without our help? As he did in the early church, today God calls us to a sacrificial kind of generosity on behalf of our pastors and our parishes. Imagine what your pastor could do if everyone's sacrifice reflected the poor widow's heart of love. He could make sure that no

brother or sister in your parish and community would ever have to go without food and medical care. He could devote more resources to the spiritual formation of the children in the parish. He could sponsor missionaries to preach the gospel to those who don't know Jesus. Our generous love for the Lord and his church could minister the gospel to thousands.

The need is great. God knows the needs of your parish perfectly. The closer you get to Jesus' heart, the more the Holy Spirit will show you how he wants you to imitate this humble widow's sacrifice. Ask him to guide you. Mark's story is not intended as a command to give away our last penny and live in poverty. We need to be responsible in our giving. Still, responsibility should not cloud God's call to be generous. When we give to God's people, we are giving to Jesus himself.

Giving from Our Poverty

St. Mark's lesson is not just a story of generosity. Jesus was struck by the difference between so many of the wealthy people, who gave from their abundance, and this woman, who gave out of her poverty. She knew that she didn't have to give her last coins to obtain God's love. She already knew that he loved her. Neither did her money help much in meeting the financial needs of the Temple. But that wasn't the point, either. She gave generously because she loved God.

Like the widow, we are all poor in different ways. Maybe you find it hard to love people outside of your family. You may not even have that much love for those in your family. Still, God asks whether you can share the little bit of love that you do have with those who need it.

Maybe you are devoid of the power to forgive. Can you tell Jesus that you will give what little mercy you have to someone who has hurt you? You may feel that you have no time because your life is so busy. Can you give just a few minutes each day to love Jesus in prayer?

God wants us to know that every gift we give—every sacrifice we make—is noticed and rewarded. His Spirit is always hovering over us, ready to respond to our generosity with an even more generous outpouring of divine love and providence. Let's give our two copper coins to God.

Rebuilding the Walls of Jerusalem

The Babylonian captivity of the sixth century B.C. had left Jeruselum in shambles. The city walls were destroyed, and the temple was reduced to rubble.

Over time, those few Jews who remained in Judah began to feel demoralized and helpless. Having been punished by God so thoroughly, they began to lose their sense of identity and, without noticing it, began to take on the habits and beliefs of the gentile peoples around them.

Eventually, word of the people's state made its way to Babylon, where some of the exiled Jews were living: "The survivors. . . who escaped exile

are in great trouble and shame; the wall of Jerusalem is broken down, and its gates are destroyed by fire" (Nehemiah 1:3). Upon hearing this, Nehemiah—an exiled Jew who had secured a position in the Babylonian court—was overcome with tears and began to cry out to the Lord. He spent the next several days in private, praying, fasting, and asking God to intervene.

Ever true to his promise, God answered Nehemiah's cry and enabled him to return to Jerusalem and those who had been left behind. Not only did Nehemiah encourage the people to rebuild the walls of Jerusalem, he began to rebuild in the people themselves the strong character that is the inheritance of every child of Abraham. Despite fierce opposition from nearby Canaanites and Samaritans, Nehemiah inspired the people of Jerusalem to devote themselves to rebuilding the city of God. No longer were they despondent and

passive. They had a future full of hope!

We live in a similar situation today. Before Nehemiah arrived, the people of Jerusalem were gripped by a spirit of malaise and passivity. Their hope gone, their minds dulled, they couldn't recognize that they were losing their faith. It took the ministry of a man who had dedicated himself to prayer and fasting to bring about a revival. Today, many of us have low expectations of what God can do in us and through us. As a result, we have become more tolerant of sin, and it has become more difficult to hear the Spirit's call to spread the gospel and build the church. This gradual decrease in our love for the Lord has had painful effects on family life. High divorce rates, increased drug and alcohol abuse—even the acceptance of something as tragic as abortion—are becoming widespread among Catholics. The spiritual walls protecting the church are weakening!

"Active" or "Passive"?

At the root of these problems is a condition of passivity. To be passive means that, instead of acting upon our environment, we allow the environment to "act upon" us. Have we allowed the philosophies and principles of our time to influence us? Do we allow the burden of building the church to fall upon someone else's—usually our pastor's—shoulders?

A person whose faith is passive will often feel beset by fears, worries, and a sense of powerlessness when faced with sin and difficulty. Such a person might pray, "Help my daughter, Lord! She is getting divorced," and feel unable to help solve the problem in any way. Eventually, that person might resign himself to the conclusion that a ruptured marriage isn't all that bad. Such conclusions show the degree to which many of our thoughts and

actions have been formed by philosophies that may be popular but are not in scripture or the teaching of the church. Beer commercials tell us that life doesn't get any better than drinking with our friends. Movies and television shows tell us that divorce and infidelity are acceptable when a person "falls out of love."

But it's not first and foremost the media that is at fault. Christians have allowed such philosophies to enter their minds. Now is the time to take action! Now is the time to reclaim our thought life and submit our desires to Jesus. During the course of our walk with the Lord, we may have come to understand the love of Christ and the power of his cross to deal with sin. We have been blessed by meeting Christ in the sacraments. Nevertheless, if we are passive, we may still believe much of what the world espouses rather than what the Lord himself teaches. If our faith is active, however, we will

be critically evaluating whether the thoughts that we carry around are consistent with the gospel.

We Can Rebuild the Walls

We can be like Nehemiah and rebuild the walls of faith. We too can take responsibility for the people of God. By fasting and praying in repentance for our sin and the sin of God's people. Although hidden from human eyes, faith-filled prayer and fasting have the power to move God's heart.

Fasting—whether from food, selfishness, or sin—is one way to make our faith active. Whatever type of fast we choose, God wants us to have a heart like Nehemiah, who mourned over his people. This type of fast requires that we have faith, love, and justice at the root of our practices. God wants us to share in his heart, which is broken over the condition of his people. We fast, not because

we are strong and we want to help our "weaker" brothers and sisters, but because we too are weak and needy before God. It is a personal cry to God that demonstrates our utter reliance on him for everything.

What do you want to do for the love of Christ this Lent? Let us offer a few suggestions. As you consider them, keep in mind your health, your responsibilities to your family, and your time. Ask the Holy Spirit to guide you into a fast that is pleasing to him. If, at any point, you find that you have slipped on your commitment, simply pick yourself up again, and start anew.

Fasting from Food

While never bound by rigid legalism, Jesus himself fasted from food (Matthew 4:2) and taught his disciples to fast as well (6:16). He knew that

such a fast can make us more reliant on God. It can teach us that "bread alone" is not sufficient to sustain our lives (4:4). When we fast from food, we give the Spirit a greater opportunity to work, not because we deserve it, but because we have made our hearts pliable before the Lord.

Fasting from Anger and Accusation

The prophets taught another kind of fast—putting away anger, dissension, and accusation: "If you remove from your midst oppression, false accusation, and malicious speech . . . then the Lord will guide you continually" (Isaiah 58:9,11). Malicious speech is one of the most destructive forces in a family or a parish community. The words that flow from our mouths often reflect the darkness hidden in our hearts. This is why fasting from accusation is so difficult for us

and yet so pleasing to Jesus. Every evening, take a few moments to examine your speech. When you recognize the times when you have spoken harshly to or about someone, ask the Spirit to show you what attitudes might lie beneath that statement. Allow God not only to forgive you for the words you spoke, but to heal you from whatever is hidden in your heart as well.

Keeping the Sabbath

Time is very valuable to us. There never seems to be enough of it. We work long hours during the week, and Sunday may be the only day we have for ourselves. Can you dedicate your Sundays to the Lord and to your family? God has promised: "If you refrain from . . . pursuing your own interests on my holy day; if you call the sabbath a delight and the holy day of the Lord honorable . . . then you shall

delight in the Lord and I will make you ride upon the heights of the earth" (Isaiah 58:13,14). This is a wonderful way to "fast"—by offering "our time" to the Lord in prayer, to our parish in service, and to our families in love.

Rather than remaining passive in Babylon while God's people in Jerusalem dwelt in shame, Nehemiah prayed and fasted. When the opportunity arose, he was ready to accept God's call to join his brothers and sisters and rebuild the walls. Nehemiah's heart so moved God that Jerusalem once more became the dwelling of the Jews and the home of the temple of Yahweh. God will do no less in you and through you this Lent. We are confident that he will guide you and draw you close as you ask him how to fast and pray.